Poems From The West Midlands

Edited by Vivien Linton

First published in Great Britain in 2009 by

Remus House
Coltsfoot Drive
Peterborough
PE2 9JX
Telephone: 01733 890066
Website: www.youngwriters.co.uk

All Rights Reserved
Book Design by Spencer Hart
© Copyright Contributors 2009
SB ISBN 978-1-84924-532-6

Foreword

At Young Writers our defining aim is to promote an enjoyment of reading and writing amongst children and young adults. By giving aspiring poets the opportunity to see their work in print, their love of the written word as well as confidence in their own abilities has the chance to blossom.

Our latest competition Poetry Explorers was designed to introduce primary school children to the wonders of creative expression. They were given free reign to write on any theme and in any style, thus encouraging them to use and explore a variety of different poetic forms.

We are proud to present the resulting collection of regional anthologies which are an excellent showcase of young writing talent. With such a diverse range of entries received, the selection process was difficult yet very rewarding. From comical rhymes to poignant verses, there is plenty to entertain and inspire within these pages. We hope you agree that this collection bursting with imagination is one to treasure.

Contents

Cubbington CE Primary School
Matthew Flavell (10) 1
Freya Rose Legon (10) 2
Mitchell Chambers (10) 3
Sylvie Ward (9) 4
Thomas West (10) 5
Nicholas Bonsall (10) 6
Darren Lingard (10) 7
Kate Bassil (9) 8
Kimberley Dunsford (10) 9

Henley-in-Arden Primary School
Adam Currien (9) 10
George Bicknell (9) 11
Lauren Bradley (9) 12
Tristan Bell (9) 13
Emily Holliday (8) 14
Danielle Trysburg (9) 15
Elena Perrins (8) 16

Henry Hinde Junior School
Laura Bowley &
Nikita Patel-Frost (10) 17
Alicia Carey &
Emily-Jean Costello (10) 18
Eloise Hadley (10) 19
Teegan Owens (10) 20
Trafford Warwick (10) 21
William Miller (10) 22
Hannah Jane Thompson (9) 23
Sophia Browning (10) 24
Christian Gasson (9) 25
Karla Bailie (10) 26
Eva Basnett & Savannah Carter (10) ... 27
Caitlin Carr (9) 28
John-Paul Woodfield (10) 29
Daniel Cole (10) 30
Robert Rice (9) 31

Jason Bond (9) 32
Ellie Hemming (9) 33
Jordan Pocknell &
Lauren Morgan (10) 34
Michael Blay (10) 35
Daniel Bloem (10) 36
Harry Machin (9) 37
Holly Newman (9) 38
Paige Lauren James (10) 39
Owen Harris (10) 40
James Humphries, Oliver Haslam &
Jack Watts (10) 41
Oliver Marks (9) & Luke Angel (10) 42
Nilum Mistry (10) 43
Ashley Bodycote (10) 44
Lauren Goodwin &
Georgia Porter (10) 45
Jacob Haycox (10) 46
Bernadette Pienaar (10) 47
Rebecca Hartopp (10) 48
Jake Evans (10) 49

Kings Caple Primary School
Morgan Harris (8) 50
Matthew Maddock (8) 51
Ben White (9) 52
Jacob Gwilliam (7) 53

Leominster Junior School
Sarah Elizabeth Fulloway (10) 54
Charlotte Chandler (11) 55
Chloe Hill (11) 56
Rachel Harris (11) 57
Ezmé Lorrimer (11) 58
Benjamin Lawrence-Howard (11) 59
Chloe Smith (11) 60
Brittany Charles (11) 61
Zoe Black (11) 62

Sophie Wilson (10) 63
Ashleigh Watkins (11) 64
Luke Scott-Fossick (11) 65
Rachel Powell Jones (11) 66
Harriet Archer-Plane (11) 67
Abigail Pugh (11) 68
Dominic Hawke (11) 69
Liam Hill (11) 70
Sam Shuck (11) 71
Jordan Acaster (10) 72
Vanessa Dawson (11) 73
Joseph Grice (11) 74
Adam Bailey (10) 75
Joe Layton (11) 76
Michael Davies (11) 77

Mordiford CE Primary School
Elizabeth Ann Windall (8) 78
Ciara Gibson (8) 79
Beth Thompson (11) 80

Our Lady of Mount Carmel RC Primary School
Tasmin Palmer (8) 81
James Walsh (8) 82
Calista Mai Lawless (7) 83
Alicja Skrycka (8) 84
Millie Gane (7) 85
Katie Ward (8) 86
Luke Hopkins (7) 87
Jack Ereaut (8) 88
Orla Lewis (8) 89
Jack Need (8) 90
Patrick McAuliffe (8) 91
Charlotte Gurney (7) 92
Ellen Cockram (7) 93
Jordan Matthews (8) 94
Emilia Shakles (8) 95
Will Noyce (7) 96
James John Tudor (8) 97
Molly Hands (8) 98
Eleanor Bowcutt (8) 99
Jack Ryan (7) 100
Joseph Smith (7) 101

Priors Field Primary School
Isabel Bush (9) 102
Molly Anne Cunnane (9) 103
Nicola Broadbent (8) 104

St Anne's Catholic Primary School, Nuneaton
Emily Taylor (11) 105
Elysia Walker (11) 106
Carlton Jorge Benjamin (11) 107
Katie Meeks (10) 108
Matthew Wright (11) 109
Brandon Walker (11) 110
Jack Bamford (11) 111
Ashleigh Atkins (11) 112

St James' CE Primary School, Hereford
Ben Jenkins (7) 113
Charlotte Perkins (8) 114
Cintia Ramos (8) 115
Drew Bass (8) 116
Edward Pritchard (7) 117
Sophia Allen (9) 118
Rees Newton-Sealy (9) 119
Honor Lewis & Izzy Moss (9) 120
Charlotte Strike (9) 121
Izzy Moss (9) 122

Westacre Middle School
Alex Narbonne (11) 123
Alexanda Raybould (11) 124
Ruth Hadley (11) 125
Ollie Bird (10) 126
Cameron James
Gerald Harrison (11) 127
Warren Hayhow (10) 128
Salome Gibson (11) 129
Samuel Thomas Dolphin Daw (11) 130
Oliver Wright (11) 131
Ethan Priest (10) 132
Junior Grenter (10) 133
Alistair Westwood (10) 134
Beth Bourne (11) 135

Jack Gandy (11)	136
Georgia Howells (11)	137
Georgie Griffin (11)	138
Emily Newman (11)	139
George Boalch (11)	140
Courtney Wallace (11)	141
Jack Packwood (11)	142
Chantal Pagett (11)	143
Jay Canning (11)	144
Brittany Wood (11)	145
Brandon Louth (11)	146
Callum Bowen (11)	147
Laura Davies (11)	148
Harry Fulloway (11)	149
Charni Jinks (10)	150
Matthew Doe (11)	151
William Dunn (11)	152
Paige Tandy (11)	153
Luke Marshall (11)	154
Georgia Knight (11)	155

Weston-under-Penyard Primary School

Josie Bailey (11)	156
Olivia Morgan (10)	157
Niles Weyman (10)	158
Holly-Anne Smith (9)	159
Joseph Fear (11)	160
Katie Marshall (9)	161
Ginnie Mellor (11)	162
Jade Smith (9)	163
Leah Franklin (7)	164
Lily Croft (8)	165
Bethany Cole (9)	166
Jack Taylor (9)	167
Rachel Robinson (8)	168
Joseph Hughes (8)	169
Morgan Smith (8)	170
Charlie Bishop (9)	171

Whitbourne CE Primary School

Alexander Everitt (11)	172
Harry Lester (11)	173
Charley Gormley (11)	174
Brett Thomas (10)	175

Whitchurch CE Primary School

Lauren Pascall (10)	176
Joseph Robins (10)	177
Thomas Howard (10)	178
Sam Robins & Michael Jode (10)	179
Claire Hughes (10)	180
Chloe Williams (10)	181

Whittington CE Primary School

Emily Jones (10)	182
Claire Davies (9)	183
George Boots (10)	184
Grace Newbrook (9)	185
Liam Yates (10)	186
Georgia Booth (10)	187
Emily Powell (9)	188
Ella Newbrook (9)	189
Callum Williams (9)	190
Matthew Evans (10)	191
Lydia German (10)	192
Tom Kilvert (10)	193
Mitch Ellis (9)	194
Olivia Griffiths-Coulthard (9)	195
Grace Meredith (9)	196
Richard George (9)	197
Hannah Ryan (10)	198
Darryl Kershaw (9)	199
Issy Budd (10)	200
Emma Arthur (10)	201
Bethany Coleman (9)	202
Lauren Edwards (9)	203

The Poems

The Beast Of Bodmin Moor

I'm prowling on the grassy moor.
My name's The Beast of Bodmin Moor.
I eat and sleep all day long,
I never do any wrong.

Some say I'm a pet cat,
Imagine me with a rat!
So when you walk on the moor,
Think about The Beast of Bodmin Moor.

Matthew Flavell (10)
Cubbington CE Primary School

Spring

Water sparkles, rests on tips of
blades of grass, as the
fascinating sun shines over
the meadow.
A dewy diamond falls from
a snowdrop, landing on the
bright, green leaves below.
Green and new twinkling shoots
of daffodils can be seen,
emerging from the damp soil.
Seeds fly, floating, fluttering on
the breezy wind.
Indigo, cream and yellow crocuses
open, say hello to the world, in
a ring around a silver birch tree.
A whispering weeping willow trails
its branches in the trickling, sky
blue stream, dancing with activity.
A bleating lamb dances, prances
and leaps across the green, green
grass on the top of a hill.
Birds cry out in song, calling
for their friends.

Freya Rose Legon (10)
Cubbington CE Primary School

Out In The African Jungles!

Elephants crash through the trees with a *boom!*
Cheetahs run through the grass with a *zoom!*

Out in the African jungles!

Lions lick up water. It lands back with a *plop!*
Buffalo wallow in the mud with a *slop!*

Out in the African jungles!

Baboons drop their fruit and *grizzle!*
Zebras sit in the sun and *sizzle!*

Out in the African jungles!

Hippos swim with a *splish, spolsh, splash!*
Crocodiles hunt with a *snap, gnash, gash!*

Out in the African jungles!

But for the first time in a century;
All goes quiet and night falls silently.

Out in the African jungles!
Out in the African jungles!
Out in the African jungles!

Mitchell Chambers (10)
Cubbington CE Primary School

Sounds Of The Ocean

Sounds of the ocean go through my head.
The *splish-splash* of the ocean tides,
The giggle of the children swimming calmly,
The chit-chat of the parents talking,
Oh it all comes through my head.

Sounds of the ocean go through my head.
The *flippety-flop* of many sandals,
The whistle of the wind blowing gently,
The *drip-drop* of the seaside showers unused,
Oh it all goes through my head.

Sylvie Ward (9)
Cubbington CE Primary School

Fun

Fun. What colour is it?
Yellow, like the sun's happy face.

Fun. What sound does it make?
Happy cheers from a football crowd.

Fun. What does it taste like?
Ice cream and jelly on a summer's day.

Fun. What does it smell like?
A summer barbecue ready to eat.

Fun. What does it look like?
Smiley-faced balloons in the sky.

Fun. What does it feel like?
Doing handstands on the soft grass.

Thomas West (10)
Cubbington CE Primary School

The African Plain

Elephants crashing through the trees,
Vultures soaring in the breeze,
Leopards scratching at their fleas,
Out on the African plain.

Hippos wallowing, having fun,
Zebras, antelopes, on the run,
Lions panting in the sun,
Out on the African plain.

Buffalo, a glossy black, many-horned team,
Cheetahs speeding like a laser beam,
Crocodiles lurking just downstream,
Out on the African plain.

Giraffes, at their enormous height,
Wildebeest charging in the evening light,
Hyenas cackling in the dead of night,
Out on the African plain.

The blood-red sun at the end of the day,
Stars twinkling faintly, far away,
Waterfalls, crashing down, throwing up spray,
Out on the African plain.

Nicholas Bonsall (10)
Cubbington CE Primary School

The Dead Of Night

The moon shining bright,
The owl singing quietly,
Careful not to wake the zombies,
The trees creaking like a door,
The wind howling violently.

The tombstones wobble,
The crows fly away,
The zombies rise,
Aarrgghh
Run away!

The ghosts and spirits block the gateway,
Demons fall from the sky,
I'm scared and worried, I start to cry,
I wake up all snug and tucked up in bed,
I realise it was just a dream.

The screaming, the chasing, the crying, the laughing,
Was that just a dream? Because it felt so real.
Was that just a dream? It was ever so vivid.
Was that a dream or did I scratch myself?
Or was it Hell?

Darren Lingard (10)
Cubbington CE Primary School

The Noise Taker
(Based on 'The Sound Collector' by Roger McGough)

A tourist called this morning
Dressed in a hula skirt
Put all the beach sounds in a bag
And rode off on her bike

The crying of dolphins
The crashing of waves
The yelling of children
As they splash in the sea

The snapping of crabs
The whooshing of whales
The squawking of birds
As they fly through the sky

The splashing of divers
The scrunching of sand
The snapping of sharks
As they look for their tea

The swishing of jellyfish
The squelching of seaweed
The slapping of stingray
As they look for their prey

The licking of lollies
The dripping of ice cream
The crunching of chips
As the people eat their fill

A tourist called this morning
Left her footprints in the sand
And left the beach in silence
It will never sound as good.

Kate Bassil (9)
Cubbington CE Primary School

Love

The colour of love is pink, like a warm blanket wrapped
around me,
The sound of love is the beautiful whispers of the ocean,
The taste of love is a sweet strawberry, full
of juice,
The smell of love is a freshly cooked chocolate cake
oozing with chocolate,
The feel of love is a warm hot water bottle snuggled next
to your chest,
Love looks like a beautiful red rose glistening in the sun.

Kimberley Dunsford (10)
Cubbington CE Primary School

Winter Is . . .

Winter is joy
Winter is misty frost
Winter is soft, white snow
Winter is frost on green grass
Winter is as cold as Mount Everest
Winter is as cold as a snowy mountain
Winter is crackling icicles falling to the ground
Winter is a thick, white blanket of snow
Winter is an enormous grey, ghostly sleigh
Winter is a big bouncing ball of snow
Winter is as cold as frost on a tree
Winter is the best thing in the world.

Adam Currien (9)
Henley-in-Arden Primary School

Nature Of Winter

Temperature going way down low,
Nipping Jack Frost on the cold, crunching snow.
Winter creates the most freezing ice on rivers,
Icy icicles on animals' shivers.
Eggs of a bird cosy in their nest.
Rippling ocean hard as a big stone chest.

George Bicknell (9)
Henley-in-Arden Primary School

Winter Wonderland

W inter is when glittery icicles fall,
 I n the winter people stand small,
 N ew white fluffy polar bears are born,
 T he people buy new clothes to be worn,
 E arth starts to become cold and hard,
 R esting cold animals in the yard.

Lauren Bradley (9)
Henley-in-Arden Primary School

A Frozen Day

W inter is as cold as ice,
I t is so cold for the poor mice,
N ice, soft snow, falling to the ground,
T he little robins flying around,
E normous icicles hang like a belt,
R ivers full of ice starting to melt.

Tristan Bell (9)
Henley-in-Arden Primary School

Winter Is . . .

Winter is hibernating hedgehogs.
Winter is white, cold, frozen logs.
Winter is treading in thick, thick snow.
Winter is feeling the north wind blow.
Winter is frost, filling up the lawn.
Winter is animals hibernating, keeping warm.
Winter is frost, making lovely white leaves.
Winter is a beautiful cold breeze swaying in the trees.
Winter is crispy icicles smashing to the ground.
Winter is soft snowflakes falling all around.

Emily Holliday (8)
Henley-in-Arden Primary School

Winter Is . . .

Winter is shiny icicles falling so slow,
Winter is robins flying high and low,
Winter is snowflakes falling as soft as a pillow.

Winter is icy icicles dripping to the ground,
Winter is snow crunching, making so much sound,
Winter is people slipping and sliding all around.

Danielle Trysburg (9)
Henley-in-Arden Primary School

Winter Is . . .

Winter is cold, white snow lying on the ground
Winter is freezing cold lakes glittering
Winter is misty days, cold as ice
Winter is a day in bed and a hot chocolate
Winter is cold ice crackling
Winter is faces red as roses
Winter is a wonderful wonderland.

Elena Perrins (8)
Henley-in-Arden Primary School

Parrot

My parrot is sleeping
He likes to fly
He's always weeping
He misses his family

He has a brother
He likes to say, 'Hello'
He misses his mother
And he misses his sister

He loves his father
He is still sleeping
His father is Arthur
He is still in a cage

He wants his family back
He really misses them
He wants to pack
And see his family again

He's so funny
He likes his mates
They give him money
He wants to move!

Laura Bowley & Nikita Patel-Frost (10)
Henry Hinde Junior School

Tiger

Mine is the head
That's no longer held high,
In the quiet evening,
As people walk by.

Mine is the face
That now frowns,
My fur has turned
A crispy brown.

Mine is the mind
That's longing to be free,
Where I dream of my jungle
Where my family should be.

Mine is the back,
All bloody and beaten,
It's been days
Since I've eaten.

Mine is the tongue,
Dehydrated and dry,
All alone at night
Is when I cry.

Alicia Carey & Emily-Jean Costello (10)
Henry Hinde Junior School

Bear

Hot bear,
Hot bear,
Forced to work for his keeper.

Chained bear,
Chained bear,
Begging for his dinner.

Unloved bear,
Unloved bear,
Crying for his forest.

Mistreated bear,
Mistreated bear,
Missing his friends.

Dusty bear,
Dusty bear,
My ted up his feet.

Eloise Hadley (10)
Henry Hinde Junior School

What Has Happened To Kitty?

What has happened to Kitty, Daddy?
What has happened to Kit?
I can't see her here, Daddy
I hope she hasn't been hit.

Why isn't she in her basket, Daddy?
Where has she run?
She's not under the cover, Daddy
Or in the baby's pram.

What has happened to Kitty, Daddy?
What has happened to Kit . . . ?

Teegan Owens (10)
Henry Hinde Junior School

Why The Animals?

Why the orang-utan?
Why the dolphin?
Why the tigers?
Why the killing?

Why the panda?
Why the wild dog?
Why the bear?
Why the cod?
Why the danger?

Why the leopard?
Why the cheetah?
Why the elephants?
Why the polar bear?
Why the destruction?

Why can't we live in peace with each other?

Trafford Warwick (10)
Henry Hinde Junior School

Chained Bear

Chained bear,
Chained bear,
Longing for the cool mountains.

Tired bear,
Tired bear,
Aching for a rest.

Sad bear,
Sad bear,
Dancing in the heat.

Scared bear,
Scared bear,
Frightened of the whip.

William Miller (10)
Henry Hinde Junior School

Why The Panda

Why us?
Why the panda?
Why choose us?
Why the hate?
Why the killing?
Why the extinction?
Why the black and white?
Why the paws?
Why the fur?
Why the panda?

Hannah Jane Thompson (9)
Henry Hinde Junior School

Tiger

Mine is the roar
Sitting in my cage
Making my throat sore
There's no more water left, it's an outrage.

Mine are the claws
On my big, padded feet
I also have a lot of sores
I've got sores from the sleet.

Mine is the roar
The roar I hear at night
I have a hurting jaw
It gives me such a fright.

Mine are the ears that hear every sound
They listen all day and all night
As I pace the ground
As I wait for the morning light.

Mine is the howl all day
And the howl all night
If I had it my way
I would use it to give people a fright.

Sophia Browning (10)
Henry Hinde Junior School

Lion

He's big and strong,
He has a giant roar,
He awakens the pride of lions
And his paws are really sore.

Claws as sharp as shattered glass,
His roar is as loud as an engine,
How slow time will pass.

I can barely sleep,
I'm thinking of sleet,
I am so furry,
I want to eat.

Christian Gasson (9)
Henry Hinde Junior School

Tiger

The tiger sleeps
And twitches its ear
All alone with
Such a big fear

You can hear him whine
As he suffers in pain
His claws all split
With a badly broken spine

The tiger with bright blue eyes
Can see them sparkle
But all in the dark
At night he cries.

Karla Bailie (10)
Henry Hinde Junior School

Leopard

How fast it sprints,
It does not go slow,
So spotty it is,
It never loses the flow!

How spotty they are,
They have crystal-blue eyes,
They can run so far,
But they have a loud *roar!*

How green the jungle is,
They are never alone,
Such sharp teeth they have,
They are always at home!

Such sparkling ears,
Such shiny teeth,
They go to sleep in fear,
They go back to the jungle, safe at home!

Eva Basnett & Savannah Carter (10)
Henry Hinde Junior School

Lion

My lion is faster
Than any master
When he roars,
He opens the doors.

He fears the light,
But loves to fight.
He has to have a moistened nose,
And if he doesn't his eyes will close.

Every year he fears I will
Leave him to pay the bill.
Now I notice he needs a shot,
But this time I'd rather not.

As he sleeps
He gives a whine.
I run upstairs
And start to cry.

Caitlin Carr (9)
Henry Hinde Junior School

Parrot

The squawk of the parrot is loud
It's trapped in a cage in a zoo
The colourful colours of the parrot are beautiful
They make you go, 'Whoo!'

Parrots make you go wild with joy
When you go, 'Whoo!' the parrot does too
When you go to the zoo
Everyone goes, 'Whoo gooo oooh!'

John-Paul Woodfield (10)
Henry Hinde Junior School

The Monkey

He sits on the floor in a cage
Playing with friends, swinging from ropes,
Getting fed by nice people
So getting some fruit is what he hopes.

He likes monkeys a lot
Sometimes they are still
Sometimes they jump about
Sometimes they just sit and chill.

Daniel Cole (10)
Henry Hinde Junior School

Snake

It lives in the dusty plains, not anymore
Hiss, it goes, in a glass cage
They come to it in a tour
It hardly grows to the size it should be

It should be free in the wild
Its cage has no sand
It tried to escape and broke scales
If they feed it they get bitten on the hand.

Robert Rice (9)
Henry Hinde Junior School

Chained Bear

Chained bear,
Chained bear,
Longing for the forest.

Lonely bear,
Lonely bear,
Dancing in the heat.

Sad bear,
Sad bear,
Aching for his home.

Whipped bear,
Whipped bear,
Forced to earn his keep.

Hungry bear,
Hungry bear,
Begging for food.

Discontented bear,
Discontented bear,
With no friends.

Ill bear,
Ill bear,
Exhausted from the work.

Stabbed bear,
Stabbed bear,
Needed no more.

Murdered bear,
Murdered bear
Forgotten in his tomb.

Jason Bond (9)
Henry Hinde Junior School

Kitty

What has happened to Kitty, Daddy?
What has happened to Kit?
I see her tray still full, Daddy
And the door is wide open
She isn't allowed out
Because she's not big enough.

Ellie Hemming (9)
Henry Hinde Junior School

Past Its Prime

Mine is the fur,
That kept me warm,
All night long,
Till the shining dawn.

Mine are the eyes
That are so bright.
Mine are the eyes,
That shone at night.

Mine are the paws,
That strolled all around
In an empty cage,
Making no sound.

Mine was the roar,
That filled with rage,
Mine is the roar,
Getting on with age.

Jordan Pocknell & Lauren Morgan (10)
Henry Hinde Junior School

What Has Happened To Kitty?

What has happened to Kitty, Daddy?
What has happened to Kit?
What if she got hit Daddy?
What if she got hit?

Why is the cat flap swinging Daddy?
Someone could have got her,
She could have run away and
A car could have squashed her.

I keep dreaming of her
Every bit of the day.
Where has Kitty gone, Daddy?
Why did she run away?

Michael Blay (10)
Henry Hinde Junior School

Chained Bear

Chained bear,
Chained bear,
Getting really hot.

Tired bear,
Tired bear,
Doing too many tricks.

Sad bear,
Sad bear,
Getting whipped.

Scared bear,
Scared bear,
People laughing at him.

Daniel Bloem (10)
Henry Hinde Junior School

Tiger

Mine is the claw
That scratches the cage,
In the dark night on the floor
Mine is the claw.

Mine are the eyes
That gaze up at the stars,
As the freezing cold wind cries
Mine are the eyes.

Mine are the legs
That used to help me stalk the prey,
In the pitch-black forest
Mine are the legs.

Harry Machin (9)
Henry Hinde Junior School

Chained Bear

Hot bear, hot bear,
Dancing all day in the heat.

Forced bear, forced bear,
Forced to work for the keeper.

Scared bear, scared bear,
Scared to make a mistake.

Chained bear, chained bear,
Begging for cool mountains.

Holly Newman (9)
Henry Hinde Junior School

Untitled

Why do you . . .
Kill me?
Hunt me?
Hate me?
Cage me?
Sell me
And
Trade me?

What have we done wrong?
What have we done to deserve it?

Why the . . .
Optimistic orang-utan?
Polar bear?
Terrific tiger?
Elephant?
Precious panda?
Bearded dragon?
Wonderful whale?

Put yourself in
All of our shoes.

Paige Lauren James (10)
Henry Hinde Junior School

Snake

It lives in the desert place not anymore.
Hiss, it goes in its cage of shiny glass.
The people come to see it at the tour.
It will grow a size not massive.

It should be free in the wild,
Not in a cage with no sand.
It tried to escape but broke scales.
If they feed it they will be bitten on the hand.

It will hiss up your hand and bite you.
Don't open the cage, it will get out and kill.
It will see a cow go *mooo!*
It will kill someone with a million.

Owen Harris (10)
Henry Hinde Junior School

The Monkey

Part of the day they sit and scratch,
They sometimes try to undo the latch.
They jump up and down acting crazy,
Then at bedtime they are really lazy.

They jump on a branch and start to swing,
You would almost think they'd sprouted a wing.
They always seem to natter and chatter,
They make a noise but it does not matter.

The male monkey is very proud,
The noise they make is very loud.
The baby monkey plays in the dirt,
The female monkey likes to flirt.

James Humphries, Oliver Haslam & Jack Watts (10)
Henry Hinde Junior School

Dogs

Mine is the bark that fills the house.
I stalk for food to fill my tummy.
I play with ball toys with my owners.
My owners feed me food that's yummy.

My nose is cold and damp.
My happy, begging eyes light up.
My fur is smooth, his face is rough.
My tail is prepared for the chase.

Oliver Marks (9) & Luke Angel (10)
Henry Hinde Junior School

Lion

How I swayed my golden mane,
But not anymore,
Because I'm not at home,
Where I left my happiness, alone.

How I roared my mighty roar,
But not anymore,
I have to keep quiet,
Otherwise the other animals go riot.

How I raced with my friends,
But not anymore,
All I do is laze around,
Or do anything that can be found.

Nilum Mistry (10)
Henry Hinde Junior School

Tiger

Your eyes light up the dull cage,
Your roar deafens me,
Your ears twitch timidly
As you listen to the keeper
Lock you in with his key.

Your paws are destroyed,
Your claws are tatters,
Your face looks distraught,
But none of the keepers think it matters.

Your tongue is dry and crispy
Desperate for a drink,
Your gums are red and sore
From chewing the cage sink.

Your nose is torn and battered
From ramming against the wall,
Your ears aren't soft and fluffy
No fur on them at all.

Ashley Bodycote (10)
Henry Hinde Junior School

Koala

Koala bears are cute but very minute
They are funny but they have a tiny tummy
They are cheeky but sometimes freaky
They are kind but they all bind

They live in a nice home but like to be alone
They don't like baboons but they listen to tunes
They are quiet but they like to go riot
They look gentle but they are really mental

They like to sleep but mostly eat
They're loving their life
So don't try and beat
So leave them alone.

Lauren Goodwin & Georgia Porter (10)
Henry Hinde Junior School

Crocodile

Crocodile, crocodile, *snap, snap, snap*,
Your eyes shine like crystals,
They don't like intruders,
You make me want to *clap, clap, clap*.

They love peace and quiet,
And not to be disturbed,
They hate people making a riot,
And want to be in the wild.

Searching for fresh flesh,
So hungry, about to die,
Floating on top of the river,
Just about to die.

Jacob Haycox (10)
Henry Hinde Junior School

Tigers

It's bad that Tiger has to live in a cage.
He is a wondrous delight.
His eyes are looking very sad.
It's like he's given up the fight.

His fur is matted and has a funny smell.
The sound of his faded roar.
He moves around, he is very weak.
He deserves a lot more.

Bernadette Pienaar (10)
Henry Hinde Junior School

Lion

I was once a high and mighty king,
Then they did this to me, I don't know why.
I was kind and giving
But they caged me.

I still have to shake my tangled mane
For the children who come to see me,
But they can't see beyond the fur.
I am going through such pain,
If only they knew.

The person who looks after me is really very lazy,
My dirty cage and lack of food
Sometime makes me crazy.
Free me, please.

Rebecca Hartopp (10)
Henry Hinde Junior School

Chained Bear

Chained bear,
Chained bear,
Tears rolling from his eyes.

Chained bear,
Chained bear,
Longing for his home.

Chained bear,
Chained bear,
Looking for some meat.

Chained bear,
Chained bear,
Hit by a bar and chain.

Chained bear,
Chained bear,
Dying in pain.

Jake Evans (10)
Henry Hinde Junior School

Happiness

Happiness is the colour of yellow,
like the bright sun on a warm, sunny day.

Happiness looks like an enormous smiley face
that somebody wears when they are happy.

Happiness feels like a fluffy, soft, white cloud
that floats in the clear, blue sky.

Happiness smells like a ball of pink petals
off a rose bush, full of sweet smells.

Happiness tastes like warm, light, milk, melted chocolate
dripping down your throat.

Happiness reminds me of happy, exciting days in the past
and it also reminds me of good days that might happen in
the future.

Happiness sounds like a little chuckle from a tiny baby.

Happiness is a *great* feeling!

Morgan Harris (8)
Kings Caple Primary School

Loneliness

Loneliness is the colour of blue,
like the deepest ocean.

It looks like a solitary grain of old rice.

It smells like a dark damp cellar,
where no one visits.

It feels like 200 iron cannonballs
pulling you down so you can't move.

It smells like dark smoke coming from a volcano
that erupted a second ago.

Matthew Maddock (8)
Kings Caple Primary School

Fear

Fear is the colour of black,
like darkness all around you in the night.

It sounds like a person screaming
in your head, like a monster.

It looks like a roaring
monster jumping at you.

It tastes like a sharp knife
cutting your mouth.

Fear is a monster taking
over your body.

Ben White (9)
Kings Caple Primary School

Anger

Anger is the colour of red,
burning fire like bubbling lava.

Anger feels like a bullet going
through your heart.

Anger smells like a bomb exploding.

Anger tastes like a bitter cherry.

Anger sounds like a gun firing.

Jacob Gwilliam (7)
Kings Caple Primary School

The Candle

T hrough the night it blazes, like the sun,
H earing whispers that no other ears will hear,
E verything cloaked in darkness except a silent glow.

C arrying its gentle load of a fading flame,
A ny blow of heavy breath and the ember will be out,
N othing stirs but the turret of red.
D anger lurks round the corner,
L ittle girls scamper up to their beds and blow,
E verything is black, and the candle is no longer aglow.

Sarah Elizabeth Fulloway (10)
Leominster Junior School

The Christmas Candle

The cold, white snow crackled,
Lying deep in drifts,
The frost bit hard;
And then I saw the candle, dimly.
I wiped the window,
Light glowed all around me,
It seemed like the sun was shining;
And then it felt like Christmas!

Charlotte Chandler (11)
Leominster Junior School

Where Is God?

Where is God?
Is He in the sun
Or sitting in the clouds?
Is He the one
Who lets people die?
Did He make me?

Children beaten . . .
Broken bones . . .
People in despair
Where is God there?

I don't think I believe
In God.
If he were real
We would not have
Sadness,
Horrible, black, windy days!

If I were God
We would have
A cleaner planet
And better times.

Chloe Hill (11)
Leominster Junior School

Climbing Hay Bluff

Floating above me
Clouds hovered
Rocks scurried down
The water stream.
The mountain will
Be waiting
So climb it
If you can.
Dark passages and
Freezing air
Breathtaking so
Do it if you dare!

Rachel Harris (11)
Leominster Junior School

Mountains

Icy water, split rocks.
The snow on the mountain, paper white, fell down softly onto the green valley below. The ragged mountain as cold as Antarctica, stood proudly over the great green valley. Thunder roared like an angry lion. Icicles hung over the jagged face of the mountain.

Ezmé Lorrimer (11)
Leominster Junior School

Poem About God

God is a fake
I could think otherwise
But it would take a lot of believing

Did He make the wonders
Of a plant in a plant pot?

Did He make me?

If He is real
He can't have time
For everyone,
That's why people die -
To keep life in balance.

Benjamin Lawrence-Howard (11)
Leominster Junior School

The Mountain

The wet, muddy, spiralling path
Getting higher and higher
Above my head,
Challenging every person
Who climbs it.
The wind howling
Around the peak,
The sharp rocks
Pointing at you in every direction.
Legs aching,
Hands numb,
The waterfall cold
And icy.
The clouds, dark
And stormy,
Looking down at the drop below.

Chloe Smith (11)
Leominster Junior School

The Mountain

It glared down at me
And shadowed all the valley
Water was running
Rocks were following.
The wind bit my face
The frost nipped my fingers
And rocks cracked
Under my feet.
The wind was howling
Water was gushing.
I inched closer to my destiny!

Brittany Charles (11)
Leominster Junior School

Climbing Hay Bluff

Stretched up into the sky
Standing tall and strong
Cold as Antarctica
The wind howling like a wolf
The ground frozen
Snowflakes fluttering
Hail dropping
The size of rocks.
The wind buffeting me
Around the narrow, slippery path
Here I finally am
At the top
Colder than ever
But still so happy!
Fingers are numb and tingling
It doesn't matter
I have made it!

Zoe Black (11)
Leominster Junior School

The Mountain

While the clouds passed by
The air became cold.
Mountain top
As high as the sky.

While the east wind blew
Snow and water fell down.
The fierce wind
In anger
Pushed back the hail
Against the high mountains.

Rocks
Slippery with water
Sky, full of dark clouds
Stretched away
Forever.

Sophie Wilson (10)
Leominster Junior School

Climbing Hay Bluff

The mountain was tall and still
Clouds surrounded it
In thin air
Snow suffocated it
The deadly sky made it colder
Rocks clutched together
Hail covered it
Wind blew fiercer than ever
Pain clings on to you
Wherever you go on it
You get breathless
Every minute of the climb
Ice cracks fast
As you try to climb over it
Worrying if you'll ever get there
Climb to the top
Feeling relieved
Knowing fair and square
You made it there!

Ashleigh Watkins (11)
Leominster Junior School

Forest Fire

Fire
Rising higher
The fire like a witch's cackle
Burnt my fence and killed my cattle.
Its deathly way burnt down the path
To farmer John's forest half.
It ripped and burned, leapt like a hound
Destroying everything it found.
Panic-stricken animals ran here and there
Even the mighty grizzly bear.
Fire
Rising higher.

Luke Scott-Fossick (11)
Leominster Junior School

The Fire

Hot fire spreads through the high woods
smoke billows up like a soaring bird, hot
fire flicks through the woods.
Fire eats the trees
bright as the sun
from a small spark
the fire
destroys the woods.

Rachel Powell Jones (11)
Leominster Junior School

The Mountain

The mountain stood there,
Straight and tall with
The sound of the birds
Singing loud and clear!

The mountain surrounded
By fluffed-up clouds,
On a winter's day
Flat rocks and
Drumlins!

The mountain peak
Covered with snow,
Little icicles, hanging
From the edge!

The mountain looked
As frozen as ever,
And needed a jumper
To make him warmer!

Harriet Archer-Plane (11)
Leominster Junior School

My Magic Box
(Inspired by 'Magic Box' by Kit Wright)

I will put in the box . . .

The Welsh dragon,
My smile from when I was a baby,
My best shoes.

I will put in the box . . .

A jumper that my great nan made,
One beautiful pearl,
Some mad magic from Merlin.

I will put in the box . . .

My wildest adventure,
A little owl,
My best friend.

My box is made of . . .
The finest pillow feathers,
The hinges are bell ropes
And the corners are lucky charms.
I shall ride with my box up to Heaven and
Show God and Jesus what I have collected!

Abigail Pugh (11)
Leominster Junior School

The Mountain

Glaring down at me
The misty clouds
As cold as ice
The stream running down
Waterfalls frozen
I could touch the clouds
How will I reach my goal?
As I climb
My breath gets taken away
No time for a break
Must keep going
To the summit.

Dominic Hawke (11)
Leominster Junior School

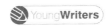

Candlelight

C hristmas is nearing
A s the days are getting shorter
N ever go out, candlelight
D ancing dreamily through the night
L ight so bright
E ver living, ever moving.

Liam Hill (11)
Leominster Junior School

Forest Fire

The fire,
Burned as bright as the sun,
Fire danced around the trees.

Fire darted up the trees,
Trees burned down into ashes,
Animals screamed in terror.

Flames ate the trees,
Trees engulfed by fire
Screamed in pain.
All that was left
Were corpses and ashes.

Sam Shuck (11)
Leominster Junior School

My Candle

An inspiring sight
The flame drawing me closer
A single ray of hope,
Lighting up the entire house
And lighting me up inside
So never let my candle blow out.

Jordan Acaster (10)
Leominster Junior School

A Winter's Candle

The snow crackled as it glistened,
The ice froze my fingers,
The wind tore me back.
And then I walked past a glowing window,
I saw a gleaming candle.

It flickered every now and again,
Dancing as it shimmered in its holder.
The flame twisted and twirled as the wax melted.
That's when it started to feel like Christmas!

Vanessa Dawson (11)
Leominster Junior School

Climbing Up Hay Bluff

The climb above me
In the cold, frozen mud
The wet grass
Soaking my feet

The soggy mud
Sticking to my feet
The water sprinkling down
To the bottom of the
Mountain

There was no flat rock
All spiky, jagged -
I was higher than God could ever be
The foggy clouds blowing in the air

It was breathtaking
Drumlins sticking up from the ground
Views glaring at me in the background.

Joseph Grice (11)
Leominster Junior School

The Bush Fire

The fire burned insanely, like Hell
As the trees ripped to shreds
The fire was like a wall of steel
The flames ripped through the trees like a cannon
The fire danced up the trees and abseiled down
The flames ran all around the jungle
Like a gorilla going ape.

Adam Bailey (10)
Leominster Junior School

Forest Fire

The fire jumped
From tree to tree
Destroying everything
In its path
Smoke covering all
The colour of misery

Like a red-hot cheetah
Flames sprinted
Through the forest
Smoke rising like an air balloon

The trees toasted
And burned
Flames lit up
The yellow sky
Scorching
Twisting
Leaving only
Ashes.

Joe Layton (11)
Leominster Junior School

The Light That Shines At Night

C alm as the air.
A s bright as the sun.
N ever fading.
D reaming all night.
L ovely sight.
E ver dancing.

Michael Davies (11)
Leominster Junior School

Beach Class

The sun beams down at her class,
The waves are crashing like a noisy room,
The palm trees are the mums waving goodbye in the wind,
The sand is the leaves blowing on the playground floor,
The fish are the children scrambling to their seats.

In their lessons their writing flows,
They have had a bad day,
They are not the only ones,
Because . . .

Bad day in the jungle,
Bad day in the sea,
Bad day in the rainforest,
Bad day for me.

The day ends with a conch shell blowing in the wind.

Elizabeth Ann Windall (8)
Mordiford CE Primary School

Bubblegum

Bubblegum, oh bubblegum, it is so sticky.
I'm always picky with my bubblegum.
I once had some bubblegum but I always swallowed it
And now I never have it.
Every time I see someone with bubblegum I get jealous.
My mum always says it's bad for me.
I do agree, it's bad for me,
But I am annoyed; she doesn't let me buy it.

All my friends make fun of me, and that's when I get sad.
For I'm not in the mood for that.
I hate my bad days that end up like that.
It's the thing I like, I thought I was nice to them,
But they don't send their niceness back!

Ciara Gibson (8)
Mordiford CE Primary School

Bad Day In The Jungle!

Ten to nine,
I hurt my spine climbing down a vine,
Tripped over a stone and broke my nose,
Ouch is how that felt!
Quarter to three,
I saw a bee and went over to say hello -
It stung me
Badly in the face, and trust me, that did hurt!
Ten to seven
I went to Heaven with memories of that day!

Beth Thompson (11)
Mordiford CE Primary School

Rabbit

R abbit running around and
A lways eating grass
B urrows in the ground going
B elow the plants
I nside and outside
T asting all of the flowers.

Tasmin Palmer (8)
Our Lady of Mount Carmel RC Primary School

Black Cat

Black cat
Is very fat,
It eats a lot of fish.
It sleeps in a bed for sleeping.
Miaow!

James Walsh (8)
Our Lady of Mount Carmel RC Primary School

Caravans

C aravans are great
A real treat to go to
R unning round and round
A lovely place to stay
V ery exciting
A lways fun to go there
N ice things to see and do
S itting outside the caravan is always fun.

Calista Mai Lawless (7)
Our Lady of Mount Carmel RC Primary School

Holidays

H ot and sunny - I am
O n holidays, lovely ice cream melting in my mouth,
L onger to play in the sunshine,
I n the swimming pool or building the sandcastles.
D ays can be full of surprises at holiday time,
A hh, so sad when I have to come back home.
Y eah, I love summertime with
S moothies, ice creams, strawberries and funny things to do.

Alicja Skrycka (8)
Our Lady of Mount Carmel RC Primary School

Summer

S itting under the shade of trees,
U mbrellas we don't need,
M int ice cream,
M mm so lovely,
E veryone can play all day,
R eady to go on holiday.

Millie Gane (7)
Our Lady of Mount Carmel RC Primary School

Snow

S lushy when the rain comes falling from the sky.
N ice and cold, good to eat when it comes by.
O h no, the sun's come out and all the snow is melting.
W *haaaa!* My best buddy is gone, Mr Snowman has melted!

Katie Ward (8)
Our Lady of Mount Carmel RC Primary School

Library

L ibraries are
I n every place,
B ringing knowledge to every
R ace. Newspapers, books or
A computer to face, why not
R ead and work in silence?
Y ou can learn at your own pace.

Luke Hopkins (7)
Our Lady of Mount Carmel RC Primary School

Rabbit - Cinquain

Jump, jump.
Come out your hole.
So you eat your carrots
And get your children or your wife.
Good boy.

Jack Ereaut (8)
Our Lady of Mount Carmel RC Primary School

Chocolate

C runch on a Crunchie
H ave a Creme Egg
O range chocolate is tasty but
C aramel's the best
O rganic is delicious
L ick your messy lips
A nd never spit it out
T aste all the flavours
E at until you pop!

Orla Lewis (8)
Our Lady of Mount Carmel RC Primary School

Holidays

H olidays are great fun
O n the aeroplane, here we go
L ying by the pool eating
I ce creams all day
D ays playing in the sun
A nd splashing into the sea
Y ellow, golden sand
S ticking to my feet.

Jack Need (8)
Our Lady of Mount Carmel RC Primary School

Patrick's Poem

My cat is a pet,
He loves to get very wet,
It came from the vet.

M um and Dad have lots
O nly to spend in shops,
N eed lots of it,
E veryone wants lots,
Y ou love it!

My first is in bee but not in tree,
My second is in jelly but not in jug,
My third is in love but not in dove,
My fourth is in small but not in stink,
My last is in you but not in loo
And sometimes I grumble!

My answer is belly.

Patrick McAuliffe (8)
Our Lady of Mount Carmel RC Primary School

Summer

S un shining high
U mbrellas we don't use
M eadows so horses can play
M eet your friends at the park
E xcited about playing
R eady to play in the fields.

Charlotte Gurney (7)
Our Lady of Mount Carmel RC Primary School

Summer

S o hot, so tired.
U mbrellas we don't need.
M uch more fun under the trees.
M mmm ice cream really tasty to lick.
E veryone is happy.
R un around and play all day!

Ellen Cockram (7)
Our Lady of Mount Carmel RC Primary School

A Great Sleep

S leeping makes me feel great
L ast to rise, I get up late
E ven when it's time for school
E yes are open but I'm no fool
P retend I'm asleep and play it cool.

Jordan Matthews (8)
Our Lady of Mount Carmel RC Primary School

Ponies, Horses And Dogs

P onies,
O n their back I love to ride,
N ever wanting to stop,
I love to groom, feed and muck out.
E veryone thinks I'm mad because I'd love to
S leep with my pony.

H orses,
O ver the hills we go
R iding, cantering, trotting and jumping,
S he loves carrots and mint treats,
E ach day we meet, I love her more.
S uch a great thing, that horse of mine.

My dog
Ruby is a puppy,
She's lively and pretty.
When she's tired she sits on my lap to sleep,
Woof, woof!

Ruby's a yapper,
She barks when she is scared.
I say, 'Shut up, Ruby, my head hurts.'

Emilia Shakles (8)
Our Lady of Mount Carmel RC Primary School

Rubbish

I am smelly and sometimes stinky
I am put out once a week
The men in the large lorry fetch me
You all have lots of it
You put it by the side of the road
Nobody wants me
What am I?

Will Noyce (7)
Our Lady of Mount Carmel RC Primary School

Acrostic Poems

Sun
S uns are very hot.
U mbrellas you don't need unless to shelter from the heat.
N o one has to stay in their homes.

Car
C ars go very fast
A s they zoom across the track,
R acing to the finishing line.

Frog
F rogs jump very high,
R ibbit, ribbit is their cry.
O h little frog, don't cry, there are loads of flies on the lily pads.
G o home little frog.

James John Tudor (8)
Our Lady of Mount Carmel RC Primary School

Chocolate/School - Haikus

Chocolate
Chocolate is the best
Chocolate always makes me smile
The best is chocolate.

School
School is really fab
My teacher is the greatest
Oh, school makes me smile.

Molly Hands (8)
Our Lady of Mount Carmel RC Primary School

Frog - Haiku

Hello slimy frog
Sitting on a lily pad
Eating a fresh fly.

Eleanor Bowcutt (8)
Our Lady of Mount Carmel RC Primary School

Riddle

I am a mammal.
I have a blow hole.
I am a predator.
I eat mostly seals.
I can swim faster than a turtle.
What am I?

Jack Ryan (7)
Our Lady of Mount Carmel RC Primary School

Summer

S ummer
U nbelievable how hot it is
M uch more ice cream for us
M ore people under the trees
E veryone's happier now
R unning, jumping, *splash,* into the pool.

Joseph Smith (7)
Our Lady of Mount Carmel RC Primary School

The Eletigercathorse

I really wanted a pet, but I didn't know what to get.
So I got an eletigercathorse.
It's got a horse's head, a cat's body, elephant's legs
And a tiger's tail.
I feed it a mixture of tuna, carrots and meat.
It's really cool, It loves splashing in the pool.
It lives in the garden shed.
I ride my pet.
But one day it ran past the building site
And she flew out of sight.

Isabel Bush (9)
Priors Field Primary School

Dogs And Gerbils

I really wanted a dog, so I bought a brown one first,
But the brown dog was not right, he kept whining in the night,
I had to get him out of sight.
I still really wanted a dog, so I bought a yellow one next,
But he was not right, he kept barking in the night,
I decided he would have to be out, out of sight.
I still really wanted a dog, so I bought a blue one next,
But the blue one wasn't right, he kept being sick in the night,
I had to get him out of sight.
I still really wanted a pet, so I caught a gerbil instead.
The gerbil was just right, he was OK in the night.
He was the perfect pet, now he's asleep in my bed.

Molly Anne Cunnane (9)
Priors Field Primary School

Munch, Munch

Munch, munch, crunch, crunch,
A little brown mouse eating its lunch,
A superstar flying in the sky,
A bright light shining into your eyes,
A mouse eating its lunch wishing for lovely things.

Flames melting in the sky like snowflakes going down in lumps,
The mouse had finished her lunch and was full,
But she could eat some more lunch,
Until she was sick,
So she kicked her leg and nicked some more food.

Nicola Broadbent (8)
Priors Field Primary School

Grandad's Birthday Treat

It was my grandad's birthday,
We thought of a treat, to take him to a restaurant
For something to eat.
We found a posh steak house,
Grandad ordered a steak.
Oh well done - chewy-chunky beefcake
(I for one thought it was a mistake)
And no sooner did he begin to eat his meat
Out jumped his false teeth,
Landing clean on his feet.
One more meat chewing by his feet
Oh Grandad, you are embarrassing me!

Emily Taylor (11)
St Anne's Catholic Primary School, Nuneaton

Who Am I?

Mini driver,
False tan wearer,
Caring helper,
Chocolate eater,
Netball player,
Year Six leader,
Big screamer,
Alcohol needer,
Fashion icon,
One of a kind.

Answer: Our teacher, Miss Finch.

Elysia Walker (11)
St Anne's Catholic Primary School, Nuneaton

What Am I?

Cold as winter snow,
Even though you may not know
It mends broken hearts,
But when it gets hot
It parts.

What am I?

Answer: Ice cream.

Carlton Jorge Benjamin (11)
St Anne's Catholic Primary School, Nuneaton

Guess Who?

Chocolate eater,
Alcohol needer,
Sarcastic driver,
Football coacher,
Coke drinker,
Peugeot driver,
Computer expert,
Fashion disaster,
He's unique.

Guess who!

Answer: My teaching assistant, Mr Lowe.

Katie Meeks (10)
St Anne's Catholic Primary School, Nuneaton

What Am I?

Sweet smeller,
Sour sucker,
Mind blower,
Eye soaker,
Tongue taker,
Face breaker,
Throat melter,
Mouth swelterer.

Answer: Sour sweets.

Matthew Wright (11)
St Anne's Catholic Primary School, Nuneaton

Penguin!

Fish taker
Tuxedo wearer
Egg keeper
Arm flapper
Slow walker
Warm cuddler
Ice skidder.

What am I?

Brandon Walker (11)
St Anne's Catholic Primary School, Nuneaton

Popcorn

I can see the popcorn blowing up in the microwave.
I can smell the sweet smell of popcorn drifting through the air.
I can hear all the popcorn blowing up ready to be eaten.
I can feel my mouth watering in desperation for the popcorn.
I am waiting to be able to taste the popcorn.

Jack Bamford (11)
St Anne's Catholic Primary School, Nuneaton

Blanket

I can see the darkness of the night sky,
the blanket that covers the Earth.
Stars give out their light,
like holes that are punctured in the blanket.

I can taste the snowflakes on my tongue,
the snow that makes a blanket over the Earth's ground.
The mother fox makes footprints in the snow.

I can feel the cold wind slapping against my cheeks,
I pull a balaclava over my face,
It forms a blanket over my skin.

I can smell the fresh night air,
it creates a warm welcoming to Jesus' people,
but is broken by violence.

I can hear the mother fox rustling in her den,
she takes some leaves to make a blanket over her cubs.
It is trampled on in the morning
because her playful cubs have . . . *awoken!*

Ashleigh Atkins (11)
St Anne's Catholic Primary School, Nuneaton

Sky

S o many different shades of blue,
K ites flying high, twisting and turning,
Y ellow ball glowing through the clouds.

Ben Jenkins (7)
St James' CE Primary School, Hereford

Holiday

H oliday, holiday, shining sun,
O cean's waves crashing on rocks.
L icking my lolly, *mmm* this is nice.
I like it here, I'll come here next time.
D ays go fast, it's nearly time to go.
A ny holiday is great to go on.
Y ou have to come here - you will like it.

Charlotte Perkins (8)
St James' CE Primary School, Hereford

Cats

C atching balls and chasing mice,
A lways busy drinking their milk.
T rying to climb a very big tree,
S cratching the curtains and sleeping in the sun.

Cintia Ramos (8)
St James' CE Primary School, Hereford

Chess

C ome and see me playing chess.
H ave you got a chessboard at home?
E ven if you find it hard, give it a go.
S it down quietly and play the game.
S ee if you can learn the moves and beat me!

Drew Bass (8)
St James' CE Primary School, Hereford

Rugby

R unning for the try,
U nder the scrum hoping to win the ball.
G etting the ball and running for the line.
B arging through the ruck.
Y es! We win the game.

Edward Pritchard (7)
St James' CE Primary School, Hereford

Green Trees

Green trees swaying in the gentle breeze,
The shady branches waving side to side
And the swishing noise that the leaves make.

Brown trees swaying in the wind,
The rough bark on the tree trunks
And how the crinkled leaves make a crispy sound.

Sophia Allen (9)
St James' CE Primary School, Hereford

The Bug House

Bug house, bug house,
Creepy, dark and smooth.

Bug house, bug house,
Wooden, brown and cosy.

Bug house, bug house,
Cosy for all bugs!

Rees Newton-Sealy (9)
St James' CE Primary School, Hereford

Beautiful Blossom

Beautiful blossom blowing in the breeze.
So silky and soft, hanging in the tree.
I'll tell you something about this tree,
It has the brightest, lightest, whitest
Blossom you will ever see.
It smells sweeter than a strawberry
And is merrier than the Queen.
It is the blossom tree.

Honor Lewis & Izzy Moss (9)
St James' CE Primary School, Hereford

Excitement!

Excitement is all the colours of the rainbow,
It tastes like candyfloss
And smells like ice cream on a hot, sunny day.
Excitement is bright lights at the fair
And sounds like children laughing and playing.
Excitement is having fun!

Charlotte Strike (9)
St James' CE Primary School, Hereford

Happiness!

Happiness is light pink
Happiness tastes like a sweet strawberry
Happiness smells like a rose
Happiness looks like a heart
Happiness sounds like the buzz of a bee
Happiness feels like having a cuddle with your mum.

Izzy Moss (9)
St James' CE Primary School, Hereford

Fear

It trembled in the darkness,
Its blank face quiet.
The thunderous pounding of its heart ringing loudly
As sweat ran down its face,
Dripping off the end of its chin.

Its nervous face, faint in the moonlight,
Worried about what there might be.
It could only see black through its eyes.
It was uncomfortable to feel.

As the thing's looming shadow crept around the corner
Ready to strike,
It ran heart beating faster than ever.
It was truly frightening.

Alex Narbonne (11)
Westacre Middle School

Love

Love is like soft rose petals on your skin
Or your vision blurred by beauty.
First kiss tasted like strawberry,
Her lips red as a rose.
Love hearts in your head and heart floating inside you
Singing love songs.
Adored by a beautiful girl.
Love is the sound banging in your chest trying to get out.
It's the smell of expensive perfume
Drawing you closer to your girl to be.

Alexanda Raybould (11)
Westacre Middle School

Sadness

Sadness is like a blue, lonely world,
It tastes as bitter as a cold-hearted drink.
It looks like a dull desert island,
A cold alley that makes you shiver,
It smells like rotted waste.
Sadness is fear.

Sadness is like a world with only you in it,
It lives at the centre of your heart.
It's like the wind blowing your hair in your face,
Staring blankly at nothing,
Sadness is like death, but worse.
Sadness is fear.

Cold-hearted blood drips from the ceiling,
Drip, drip, drip onto your clothes.
It's like losing a close friend or family,
Sadness is blue and grey.
Sadness is fear.

Ruth Hadley (11)
Westacre Middle School

Hate

Hate, eating away at your feelings
Like a bee stinging in your heart,
It smells like cheese moulding in the fridge,
Or a bull bombarding through a village.

Hate, mysteriously piercing a black hole in your heart,
Rapidly wrapping a deer in a wood,
All you can hear is the bull smashing bottles.

Hate, smiling a victorious smile,
Rudely blushing through the doors of a hospital,
You can taste the blood on your lips.

Hate.

Ollie Bird (10)
Westacre Middle School

Laughter

It sounds like people having fun,
It tastes like happiness flying everywhere,
It smells like air,
It looks like air coming out of an aeroplane in the sunny sky,
It feels like it tickles inside,
It reminds you of an ongoing laughter.

Cameron James Gerald Harrison (11)
Westacre Middle School

Love

It sounds like joy and lots of birds singing.
It tastes like heart-shaped sweets and it makes your heart beat.
It smells like champagne, chocolates, wrapped for delight.
It looks like you're in Heaven where an angel fired an arrow
 into you.
It feels like you are going to burst with passion.
It reminds me of when you're with your mum having a fun time
 together and whenever.

Warren Hayhow (10)
Westacre Middle School

Happiness!

It sounds like people jumping up and screaming from the top of their voices.
It tastes like a big bowlful of delight.
It smells like desire when you're under the spotlight.
It feels like a comfortable bed when you're about to drop.
It looks like a kitten prancing around.
It reminds me of Drayton Manor!

Salome Gibson (11)
Westacre Middle School

Darkness

It creeps up on you
And takes your sight away.

It works its way into your mind
And messes with your feelings.

It tickles your senses,
It destroys your heart
And smashing your skull.

Samuel Thomas Dolphin Daw (11)
Westacre Middle School

Fear

I taste of eyeballs and rotten flesh,
I am a black pinch of darkness,
I am a scary monster under your bed,
I can be scarier than a zombie,
I can throw darkness in your face,
I am death in your dreams.

Oliver Wright (11)
Westacre Middle School

Anger

It sounds like a low growling noise.
It tastes like bitter, mouldy cheese.
It smells like a burning fire getting hotter and bigger,
Destroying everything in its path.
It looks like a bright red shadow about to explode.
It feels like a violent erupting volcano.
It lies asleep until something wakes it,
Then it begins to bubble and shake in the bottom of your belly.
As it gets bigger it builds up until it has no more space
So it has to come out as an eruption of violent words
Straight out of your mouth.
It reminds me of a car explosion and a lion's roar.

What am I?

Ethan Priest (10)
Westacre Middle School

Fear

Fear is a man
Blocking your path,
Waiting for you to walk back.

Following every step you take
Even in your sleep.

Fear is a shadow in the dark,
But when you lose it
It'll be back to haunt you.

Fear is a man that puts you in a cage
Until you realise there is no need to be scared,
So now you can break through.

Now the man is no more.

Junior Grenter (10)
Westacre Middle School

Sadness

Sadness is blue,
The colour of tears,
The tears that run down your face,
Like an athlete running his favourite race.

Sadness is grey
Like a dull, desolate island,
Like a human weeping
In the dark corner.

Sadness is colourless
Like a brainwashed child,
Sadness is stalking you and I,
Waiting,
Waiting to wash the colour out of us.

Sadness is pathetic,
Thunderous and fearful,
It will go to all edges of the world to grab you,
To make you one of its own.

Sadness is blue,
The colour of tears.

Alistair Westwood (10)
Westacre Middle School

Hate

Hate is black in the dark night,
Strong as a devil's flame,
Hate lives in a dark, eerie alley,
Behind a misty wood.

Hate is mean,
Vicious as could be,
Hate becomes jealousy,
The face of an enemy.

Hate represents the future
For an unhappy life,
Hate is like a dark raincloud
That never moves away.

Hate is hurtful
Like a hot gas stove,
Hate is like
The face of a devil's eye.

Beth Bourne (11)
Westacre Middle School

Sadness

Sadness is blue,
The colour of tears.
Sadness is weeping
And crying in the corner.

Sadness is grey,
Dull and dark.
Sadness is fearful,
Murderous in the right hands.

Sadness is colourless
Like death stalking every corner.
Sadness is thunderous,
Aggressively dragging you to Hell.

Sadness is brown
Like a tree moving in the wind.
Sadness is pathetic,
Tearful and outspoken.

Sadness is blue,
The colour of tears.

Jack Gandy (11)
Westacre Middle School

Love

As I picked up my cocoa
And drained it in my mouth,
After my mum gave me a hug
This left a warming feeling inside me
As I went upstairs and jumped into bed.

As the sun rose
I woke up smiling
With a tingle inside me,
Knowing that my family
Are not that far away.

Mum comes into my room
And gives me a warming kiss,
She gives me some cocoa
And tells me to get ready for school.

After school I get loved some more,
Meeting my dog at the very door,
She licks me all over my face.
Love can be broken but only in space.

Georgia Howells (11)
Westacre Middle School

Love

Love feels like a soft pillow waiting to be hugged.
Love is smooth and silky.
When love is touched it feels warm and welcoming.
Love feels wonderful.

Love looks like a soft bed of roses.
Love looks calm and quiet.
When love is seen, it brings happiness and joy.
Love looks wonderful.

Love tastes like sweet rose Turkish delight.
Love is sugary and sweet.
When love is tasted it lasts for 1,000 years.
Love tastes wonderful.

Love smells like a new brand of rose perfume.
Love smells flowery and fruity.
When love is smelt it brings a sweet scent.
Love smells wonderful.

Love sounds like birds tweeting.
Love sounds soft and cheerful.
When love is heard it's fresh and new.
Love sounds wonderful.

Georgie Griffin (11)
Westacre Middle School

Sadness

Sadness is tears,
Tears streaming down your face.
It wraps you up
And won't let go.

The sorrow that lies beneath you
Is all due to sadness.
Sadness is always there,
Like a stalker
Who's there wherever you go.

It's like a dog
That is desperate for love
So it follows you everywhere,
Every minute of the day.
That's sadness,
It's a lot like it.

I believe in sadness,
I believe that it's there,
Wherever you turn,
Left or right,
It's always there.

Emily Newman (11)
Westacre Middle School

Devastation

A stampede of rushing wildebeest
Charging through a crowded street.
Vandals hiding in the shadows,
Seeking revenge.
Blood dripping from the gutters of an abandoned house
In an abandoned street.

Ghosts and ghouls hide around corners,
Waiting for someone to pass.
Smashed glass scattered all over the floor,
With tarantulas under every nook.

Earthquakes and fire cause devastation,
In a field of rubble
Which used to be the city of Worcester.
Bodies lying on the floor
And injured, squealing babies
Who only just survived.
Arms and legs scattered on the floor
And mothers calling for their children.

Chaos as hairy wolves
Search for their prey,
This happens in the night, not in the day.

George Boalch (11)
Westacre Middle School

Darkness

D arkness goes wherever it chooses.
A venging souls screaming, pleading with him
R oaming through black Earth as wolves,
K illing people and making sure that they are dead.
N othing can stop it.
E volution, it hurts horrified children screaming.
S creaming parents worried for their children.
S creaming children hoping to get home before the darkness
                                             gets them.

Courtney Wallace (11)
Westacre Middle School

Darkness

D eath combined with pain
A venging knights slashing heads
R ampaging
K illed rat on the side of the road
N obody around in the dark town
E ating fiery coal
S adness all around the house
S lashing swords clash.

Jack Packwood (11)
Westacre Middle School

Hunger!

It is the sight of all the poor
Children with swollen bellies
With a rumble in their tum.
That's how I feel when I
Haven't eaten for a few hours.

Chantal Pagett (11)
Westacre Middle School

Hunger

H uman cruelty, people underfed and people who are even dead.
U nderstanding people die from being starved not far from death.
N ot much hope of survival as their desire for food
   becomes greater.
G reater and greater people's appetites become as they
   turn inhuman.
E ager people become for food before their death becomes
   a reality.
R aging people like animals seek for food before their death
   becomes a reality.

Jay Canning (11)
Westacre Middle School

Happiness

H appiness is the best thing that people
and children can have in the whole world.
A nger is the worst, when you fall out with people.
P eaceful people with their friends.
P layful children playing with their delightful parents.
I ntelligent children asking for help.
N oise is beautiful as children are singing with joy.
E xploring children and parents rushing around, skipping in the park.
S creaming children running around having a great time with their friends.
S mart children walking to school with their friends.

Brittany Wood (11)
Westacre Middle School

Darkness

D emons surrounding the forest, ravenous for blood.
A bandoned people drenched in blood.
R avenous demons looking for dead people to suck their blood till death.
K iller vampires searching for blood everywhere around the forest.
N ervous people waiting to die in peace.
E xcruciating pain with the sound of bones snapping in half.
S cary people sprinting around the dark forest.
S leepless people dying from loss of blood.

Brandon Louth (11)
Westacre Middle School

Darkness

D emons destroying innocent victims
A bnormal screams come from the shadows
R aces of rats bring plague to the unsuspecting victims
K idnapped children shriek aloud
N ever visit this place 'trespassers will be eaten'
E verybody had nobody
S hadows cloud the city
S ilence is all you will hear for the darkness is everywhere.

Callum Bowen (11)
Westacre Middle School

Darkness

The blackness in the pitch dark of the cave,
Nowhere to go,
Stuck in a cave,
Frightened.

The shadows calling, with their souls
All around you,
Yet nobody is there.

You have run away from your family,
Lost in the cave, wanting to go back.

You're lost.
Suddenly you see a light.
Then you are in the forest
With the wolves howling, like lions roaring.

Lost in the forest.
Scared, frightened.

The darkness, is what you have to be frightened of!

Laura Davies (11)
Westacre Middle School

Darkness

It creeps, it crawls like zombies' hands,
Reaching out for death,
It yells, it screams like death
Approaching on a black horse,
Don't let it free,
It will spread with glee,
But nothing will stir again,
It will go down, in *darkness*.

Harry Fulloway (11)
Westacre Middle School

Darkness

It flows through the air like a torched ghost
Howling like the wolves.
The blackness calling after you
Like a screaming nightmare.
It smells like death approaching.
It looks like a bat scorching through the caves.
Darkness, it's terrifying,
Never let it free.

Charni Jinks (10)
Westacre Middle School

Anger

It is like a ball of fire destroying a house.
It is a lion's roar or the squeak of a mouse.
It is as tall as the sky but extremely red.
It is the opposite of nice and close to dread.
It is like a dragon, angry and feared.
It is like a puzzle, both strange and weird.
It takes the niceness out of your soul.
What takes its place is a big, black hole.
It is like a bottle bubbling with rage.
It is like a monster trapped in a cage.

Matthew Doe (11)
Westacre Middle School

The Anger Poem

It sounds like a groan or a high-pitched squeak.
It smells like a burning fire destroying everything in its path.
It tastes like mouldy cheese.
It looks like bright red shadows about to explode.
It feels like an erupting volcano which lies asleep until something wakes it.
Then it begins to bubble and builds up until it comes out as an eruption of words out of your mouth.
It reminds me of a car exploding, a volcano erupting
and a lion's roar.

William Dunn (11)
Westacre Middle School

Anger

It is a low roar or a growling voice.
It tastes like a mouldy, gross loaf of bread.
It smells like a burning forest getting hotter and hotter every hour.
It looks like a man about to explode with fire.
It feels like my hands are burning up when I touch it.
It reminds me of a lion's roar and a volcano erupting.

Paige Tandy (11)
Westacre Middle School

Darkness

It is like a shadow creeping up behind you
and swallowing the light from around you,
It sounds like a hissing snake catching its prey,
It smells like mice rummaging through the dustbins,
It tastes of bitterness when you're all alone,
It feels like tickling fingers resting on your shoulders,
It looks like a vampire begging for your blood,
It reminds me of the sea swallowing its victim to the
soft, sandy bed.

Luke Marshall (11)
Westacre Middle School

Shadows

Somewhere down that dark street,
Somewhere down that road,
Somewhere along that gloomy alleyway,
Deathly shadows lurk.

Waiting for villainous revenge,
They crouch ready to pounce,
Like a flea-ridden cat, starving and bedraggled.
Ravenous and intimidating,
The murderous shadows wait.

Not even the bravest warrior
Dares to glance down this death-stricken street.
Spiders tremble on their cobwebs,
Waiting to watch the next bloody murder.

Blood splatters up the once graffiti covered wall,
A tattered carcass lies still among the decaying rubbish.
Something is slopping on fresh, raw meat,
A creature has been devoured tonight,
By the ever ravenous, deadly *shadows*.

Georgia Knight (11)
Westacre Middle School

Winter Thoughts

Snowflakes in the air,
Children stop and stare.
Their lit up faces shine and glow
As drops of rain turn into snow.
Everyone's in a good mood,
Fat from Christmas food!

The morning sun will rise
Into white and misty skies.
There are sounds of some birds singing
And distant church bells ringing.
The break of dawn has come,
A new day, lots more fun!

Winter has arrived,
All lucky birds survived!
They look forward to a time they know
When there is no longer threat of snow.
Summer lies ahead,
No freezing cold to dread!

Josie Bailey (11)
Weston-under-Penyard Primary School

White Winter

Blowing here and there,
As children stop and stare,
A gust of ice cold wind,
Through trees already thinned
Of all their autumn leaves
By Jack Frost's winter thieves!

Olivia Morgan (10)
Weston-under-Penyard Primary School

Wintertime

Snow is falling fast,
Autumn now has passed,
From crunchy leaves to glistening snow
That gives off such a shiny glow!
Footprints that we stepped,
Covered while we slept.

Niles Weyman (10)
Weston-under-Penyard Primary School

A Winter Day

The day is nearly here,
The break of dawn is near.
Wind whistles in the trees,
'Come on morning, come here please!'
Soon the day will break,
I'll ice skate on the lake!

The day has finally come
With the dawn of morning sun!
Children playing all around,
Skidding ice skates on the ground,
Happy voices, what a sound!
Hot chocolate costs a pound!

Holly-Anne Smith (9)
Weston-under-Penyard Primary School

Wintertime

Snowflakes falling to the ground
Children playing all around
They hope the snow will stay
It's come to the end of the day
The snow is fading away
Poor Billy wants it to stay!

Joseph Fear (11)
Weston-under-Penyard Primary School

The Rather Thin Snowman

As I run around
Through thick snow on the ground,
My hands and toes are getting cold.
But what a shame when I am told
It's time I must come in.
My snowman's rather thin!

Katie Marshall (9)
Weston-under-Penyard Primary School

Wonderful Winter!

Snow falls thick and fast,
I really hope that it will last!
Happy children's faces glow
As they make their footprints in the snow.
It's getting really cold,
Lots of hats and gloves are sold!

The sun will soon arrive,
The snow will not survive.
Now the birds will come out,
But you'll not hear the children shout.
The snow's all gone away
Until another day!

Ginnie Mellor (11)
Weston-under-Penyard Primary School

Who Am I?

Banana muncher
Brother liker
Sister lover
World's writer
Man U maniac

Answer: Bethany.

Jade Smith (9)
Weston-under-Penyard Primary School

Little Sister

That's my little sister, she is one year old,
And she's so cute,
I always like to hold her.
That's my little sister,
She is surely not to be sold,
She is as precious as gold.

Leah Franklin (7)
Weston-under-Penyard Primary School

Who Am I?

Cat lover
Clever thinker
Brother hater
Strawberry liker
Great believer
Apple muncher
Story reader
Good helper
Lily tickler
Glasses wearer
Fantastic sew-er

Answer: Harriet Aubrey!

Lily Croft (8)
Weston-under-Penyard Primary School

Who Are They?

They are strict and can be nice
They are loud but can be quiet
They do maths and English
They tell people off and give people stickers
They do lots of jobs and go on the computer
Who are they?

Answer: Teachers.

Bethany Cole (9)
Weston-under-Penyard Primary School

The Who's Who Of The Horrible House

Inside the horrible house
There is a big black bat biting
And a freaky, fiery fighter fighting.
A gigantic jade giant jumping
And a creepy khaki kangaroo kickboxing.
A scary silver skeleton screeching
And a vicious violet Viking vanishing.

Jack Taylor (9)
Weston-under-Penyard Primary School

Cat Flap

My cat uses a cat flap,
Flap, flap, rap, tap, rap, tap,
That's how it goes.
It flaps and it blows.
Flap, rap, flap, pop,
That's how it goes.

Rachel Robinson (8)
Weston-under-Penyard Primary School

The House Of Horrible Monsters, Keep Out!

Inside a dark, old, creepy house
Are blue, red, green, orange,
Silver and purple *monsters!*
Which means vampires, snakes,
Ghosts, bats, hairballs, wolves,
Gnomes and other monsters.
They sleep in the day
And wake up at night,
So when you are in bed -
Watch out!

Joseph Hughes (8)
Weston-under-Penyard Primary School

The Children In The Playground

Three bored children
Didn't know what to do,
One ran off
And then there were two.

Two bored children,
One was done,
Then three was one!

One bored child having fun,
Then she skipped off
And then there were none.

Morgan Smith (8)
Weston-under-Penyard Primary School

Who Am I?

Sister lover
Spider hater
Man U lover
Boy liker
Apple liker

Answer: Jade Smith.

Charlie Bishop (9)
Weston-under-Penyard Primary School

Dear Moon

Dear Moon,

Just a line to say
Thanks for this
And every day.
Lunar eclipses
And the tides,
Even aliens
May be living on your other side!
Your puzzling character,
As silent as space,
Keeping us wondering
If you have another face.
Please carry on,
We know your worth,

Love from a friend
From planet Earth.

Alexander Everitt (11)
Whitbourne CE Primary School

Thank You, Fields

Dear Fields,

Just a line to say
Thanks for this
And every day.
Your corn and wheat
Are very nice,
Along with
Your scrummy rice.
On summer days
Hay fever roams
Around the air,
Making us stay in our homes.
Please carry on,
We know your worth,

Love from
A friend on planet Earth.

Harry Lester (11)
Whitbourne CE Primary School

A Thank You Letter

Dear Rain,

Just a line to say
Thanks for this
And every day.

Your rain falls and raindrops
Are just as great,
Sometimes you're shining,
Here you are in the lake.

On dismal days,
As clear as a mate,
In a cloud
You calmly wait.

Till out you sail
With cheerful fate,
Like a baby wails
Going to a fete.

To put some water
On the whole world's face,
Thanks for those cheerful
Raindrops, mate.

Love from
A friend on planet Earth.

Charley Gormley (11)
Whitbourne CE Primary School

Dear Water

Dear Water,

Just a line to say
Thanks for this
And every day.
As I turn on the tap
You come in a rush,
I want to drink you,
You look so lush.
Now it's rain,
When you come so drippy,
You even go into
The Mississippi!
When you come
You are so cold,
All the cars
Get put on hold.
You shine like silver
In the sun,
Giving precious life
To everyone.
Please carry on,
We know your worth,

Love from
A friend on planet Earth.

Brett Thomas (10)
Whitbourne CE Primary School

Freaky, Forbidden Classroom

I discovered something in my freaky, forbidden classroom . . .
I heard a sudden bang coming from inside,
As I went to investigate I nervously tried
Not to think about it, but the rattling bang
Kept going on and on like a whirlwind.
I felt a warm breath going down my back,
Like a slithering snake.
I anxiously went on looking around
Like a hawk waiting for its food.
I saw the dragon on the wall wave to me
And whisper a ghostly threat.
I suddenly looked down, I saw the witch's deep blue eyes
Trying to hypnotise me.
I then heard a deadly voice say, 'You are not alone!'
I turned, looked at the whiteboard
And there it was written in black and white.
I could feel my face turn pale white.
I twirled around like I was dancing,
I saw a shadow lurking in the corner.
I wasn't alone . . .

Lauren Pascall (10)
Whitchurch CE Primary School

A Spook's Tale!

Eyes glowed,
Clocks whirled,
Goosebumps grew
And globes twirled.
Paper tore,
Drawers slid,
Blood dripped
And vampires hid.
Lights flickered,
Curtains shook,
Heard footsteps approach,
I couldn't bear to look!
Doors slammed,
Pictures fell,
Voices echoed,
They were creatures from Hell!
At midnight!

Joseph Robins (10)
Whitchurch CE Primary School

The Devil's Classroom

I heard the door slam behind me like I was bewitched.
I felt like an abandoned orphan.
I heard the door creak like a cat looking for a mouse,
I saw the clock spin like it was watching me.
I looked at my watch there and saw a face crying blood,
I noticed ghastly goosebumps gradually growing up my arm,
I heard footsteps coming towards me.
I saw blood writing saying, 'Hell's gates opening to come for you.'
I saw blood dripping down the walls, like trickling tears.
I feared the end may be nigh.

Thomas Howard (10)
Whitchurch CE Primary School

Robin Hood

Robin Hood isn't very good,
He stole from the poor to go on a grand tour.
His merry men stole a hen for their brother Ben.
Maid Marion drank some sherry, then her belly got so hairy.

Robin Hood had a hood which wasn't very good.
He found wood and understood it wasn't very good.
He had a bow that went so slow he could not be bothered to shoot,
Because he had a root in his boot.

Sam Robins & Michael Jode (10)
Whitchurch CE Primary School

The Haunted Classroom

I heard the pencils and pens click together and snap,
I noticed the deep drawers open and shut
As if they were alive.
I discovered that the globe fell
Without a hand to push it.
I gazed at the pale face on the whiteboard,
I knew at once I was not alone.
I stared at the hand reaching out of the board,
I heard footsteps behind me.
I felt a warm breath down my back.
I flung my body round like a ball of fire,
I didn't see anyone, however hard I looked.
I felt fingernails running rapidly up my back . . .

Claire Hughes (10)
Whitchurch CE Primary School

Penguin At School

I met a penguin
On the way to school,
I couldn't help it,
I thought it looked so cool.
It had no name so I called it Bit,
I took it into school,
Hid it in my locker,
Even though it broke the rule
'Cause we weren't allowed pets in school.

Chloe Williams (10)
Whitchurch CE Primary School

The Four Seasons

Winter, in the cold outside,
Grey clouds form together,
The trees have already died,
The sky as black as leather.

Spring, daffodils start to grow,
As the church bells ring,
The sky turns blue very slow,
Bluebells start to ping.

Summer, hot sun
Fills the air with warmth,
As bunnies run,
It feels like there is never going to be a storm.

Autumn, the leaves turn colour
As they also fall off trees,
The sky is duller,
Back to the hive go the bees.

Emily Jones (10)
Whittington CE Primary School

The Countryside

On a lovely sunny day
The sun was blazing,
Cows were grazing,
Grass was waving.

Rivers were swirling,
Trees were whirling,
Clouds were twirling,
Bees were buzzing.

Wind was whispering,
Leaves were twisting,
Birds were tweeting,
People were eating.

Claire Davies (9)
Whittington CE Primary School

The Beast

T erritory's beast
I nvades people's homes
G reat and powerful
E ager to pounce for his prey
R are to find.

George Boots (10)
Whittington CE Primary School

A Field Full Of Flowers

A field full of flowers, all I can see,
Daisies and tulips surrounding me.

A field full of colours, yellow and green,
The most colourful painting I have ever seen.

A field full of smells, as lovely as ever,
You'll never get anything smelling like this, never.

A field full of taste, lovely and sweet,
Almost tastes like some bread with wheat.

A field full of sound, fills my ears,
Just like the music on the piers.

A field full of memories, for now I leave,
A field full of everything where I've been.

Grace Newbrook (9)
Whittington CE Primary School

Boo

I've got a dog at home called Boo,
To look after her there's always something to do.
Take her for walks and scratch her belly,
Oh, and one last job that's rather smelly.
It's the job I hate to do,
That's right, it's picking up poo!

Liam Yates (10)
Whittington CE Primary School

Teachers - Haiku

They are stern but kind
Only shout if you've done wrong
Just like the teachers.

Georgia Booth (10)
Whittington CE Primary School

The Dragon

The dragon waits in his creepy lair,
He'll hunt you down so soon.
His least favourite food is a pear,
So he orders his cheese from the moon.

The dragon will wrap you up in rope,
Hundreds of knots, oh so tight,
Then he'll cover you up in soap
And leave you there all night.

The sun comes up, he'll ready the pot
With water from mountain streams,
His breath will make it nice and hot,
The thought will make you scream.

He'll put on his chef's apron and hat
And invite all his best friends too,
I'm not sure what you'll think of that
Because the main course will be you!

Emily Powell (9)
Whittington CE Primary School

Summer

Summer is sunny
And I've got my money
To spend on a nice holiday.

It would be nice
If I had some ice
To go in a very cold drink.

My mother nags me
To bring my bikini
So I can go in the sea.

This is it, we are on the plane!
We're going to lovely, boiling hot Spain.
I hope we have a nice time there.

A five star hotel, wow, that's good!
I hope the park is not full of mud
Like back in England.

I get into the pool
The sun is shining like a jewel
I am hot, the pool is cool.

Ella Newbrook (9)
Whittington CE Primary School

Neon Tiger

You're a brave adventurer
In search of the rare *neon tiger!*
There is a dark jungle
With loads of creatures.
If you step in the very dark jungle
You'd better be careful!
You see monkeys, snakes and birds.
But you want something else.
You search deep in the jungle.
When your hopes are down
You see it, the *neon tiger!*
Your quest is not over though,
You still need to get out of there, *alive.*
You run as quickly as you can,
You trip, everything goes black.
You wake outside the jungle.
You're really confused but you don't care
Because you found the *neon tiger!*

Callum Williams (9)
Whittington CE Primary School

My Pigeons

There once was a pigeon called Boris,
Who lived with a pigeon called Doris.
They made a nice nest
And did their best.
They laid two eggs, all white,
And sat on them day and night.
Eighteen days later they hatched,
Just like twins, they matched.
They fed them on seeds
And also on weeds
And lived happily ever after.

Matthew Evans (10)
Whittington CE Primary School

Whizzy Lizzy

Whizzy Lizzy was so whizzy.
She would run through obstacles
And round twisty bends,
Up mountains and round curly trees,
But one day she could not do
Any tricks such as these,
Poor whizzy Lizzy.

She went down a mountain
And bumped her head on a fountain.
Now poor Lizzy was so dizzy. *Boohoo*.
So she went to bed and she was snoring,
Snoring so much she
Could not get up in the morning.
Poor dizzy Lizzy.

Later, when she went to school,
All she could do was sit and drool.
Even later she fell off her stool.
Poor dizzy Lizzy.

When she got home there was a letter
From the doctor, it spelled 'get better.'
So with rhythm and rhyme
And magic and time,
Lizzy went from dizzy back to whizzy.

Lydia German (10)
Whittington CE Primary School

Man U

M anchester United is the best
A rrival of the year
N ani is one of the top ten players

U nited, everybody supports.

Tom Kilvert (10)
Whittington CE Primary School

The Fat Cat

There was a fat cat called Matt,
All he did was sit on the mat.
One day he decided to go through the cat flap,
But fat Matt got stuck in the cat flap,
Poor, fat Matt.

Mitch Ellis (9)
Whittington CE Primary School

Summer

S ummertime is really hot. I am sat
U nder the parasol, eating ice cream.
M um and Dad love to sunbathe in the sun,
M um is turning golden-brown.
E verybody is having fun,
R ight now I am really happy.

Olivia Griffiths-Coulthard (9)
Whittington CE Primary School

The Ghost

The ghost hovers through the hall.
The ghost is like a white sheet.
'Boo!' it shouts from room to room,
Until the morning comes.

Grace Meredith (9)
Whittington CE Primary School

School

Firstly, take a hint of totally chatty children,
Whisk with some hilarious headmasters.
Secondly, take a pinch of tremendous teaching.
Thirdly, take a bag of brains,
Stir with a teaspoon of incredible intelligence,
Blended with know-it-all knowledge,
Mix with satisfactory sport.
Next, take a handful of loony literacy,
Beat with stupid spellings,
After that fold with funny fighting.
Pour in some perfect PE,
Add some marvellous maths
And rub in some fantasy fractions.
Bake in some scalding soccer,
Serve with some ridiculous RE.

Richard George (9)
Whittington CE Primary School

The Silent Dragon

There is a dragon who lies in a cave,
For that was once his home;
But now his home has become a tomb,
As he has died alone.

Knights and soldiers told the tales
About how hard they fought;
How they tried to cure the town of its fears,
That the mighty beast had brought.

This majestic creature ruled the skies,
The land and shining seas;
And in the skies while he swooped and soared,
What an amazing sight to see.

But as time went on,
Unable to defend,
This beast got weak and old,
But familiar to the end.

Hannah Ryan (10)
Whittington CE Primary School

Ice Cream

I cy cold
C atches the back of your throat
E aten on a hot day

C reamy smooth
R ounded into a cone
E verybody loves it
A ll flavours
M mm, that's good.

Darryl Kershaw (9)
Whittington CE Primary School

Best Friends

Best friends here,
Best friends there,
Some best friends are everywhere!

Some keep secrets,
Others tell lies,
Most of your friendship never dies.

We all have friends
That care for us.
When they do
You feel your heart starting to fuzz!

Issy Budd (10)
Whittington CE Primary School

Stars

Stars so bright
Like the light,
Very high up
In the dark of the night.

Shining down
On the world tonight,
They are like golden bright
Shining lights up above.

As we lie in bed
They are on duty
Just for the night,
As they shine so bright!

Emma Arthur (10)
Whittington CE Primary School

Shopping!

I'm going shopping again!
'Quick,' says Mum.
I ran down the lane,
I jumped on the bus.

I'm going shopping again,
I'm going shopping again.

We've arrived at the shop
And Mum's got out her list.
We've got to get fruit, veg and a mop.
How will we manage to carry the lot?

I'm going shopping again,
I'm going shopping again.

We made our way to the till.
One by one, items are scanned,
Mum nearly faints when she has the bill.
'Oh well,' she says, 'we won't tell Dad!'

Bethany Coleman (9)
Whittington CE Primary School

School

S chool is fun for me
C ross-country makes me tired
H all assemblies can be fun
O llie, the dog, comes and says hello to Year 5
O ccasionally we have lunch outside
L ydia is my best, best, best friend in school.

Lauren Edwards (9)
Whittington CE Primary School

Young Writers Information

We hope you have enjoyed reading this book - and that you will continue to enjoy it in the coming years.

If you like reading and writing poetry drop us a line, or give us a call, and we'll send you a free information pack.

Alternatively if you would like to order further copies of this book or any of our other titles, then please give us a call or log onto our website at www.youngwriters.co.uk.

Young Writers Information
Remus House
Coltsfoot Drive
Peterborough
PE2 9JX
(01733) 890066